The OpenAI o1 Models
The Rise of Machine Intelligence

An Exploration of Their Capacity and Breakthroughs in Solving the Unthinkable

Roger A. Shawn

Copyright

Copyright © Roger A. Shawn. All rights reserved.

No part of this publication may be reproduced, distributed, or transmitted in any form or by any means, including photocopying, recording, or other electronic or mechanical methods, without the prior written permission of the publisher, except in the case of brief quotations embodied in critical reviews and certain other non-commercial uses permitted by copyright law.

Table of Content

Copyright.. 2

Table of Content.. 3

Introduction.. 5

Chapter One... 8

The Evolution of AI Technology................. 8

Chapter Two.. 15

What Makes the o1 Models Unique............ 15

Chapter Three... 24

Applications Across Disciplines................ 24

    Revolutionizing Scientific Research.................. 24

    The Role in Healthcare..................................... 29

Chapter Four... 34

Coding and Multi-Step Workflows............ 34

Chapter Five.. 39

The Economic Divide: Preview vs. Mini..... 39

Chapter Six.. 49

Limitations and Drawbacks..................... 49

Chapter Seven.. 54
Safety and Security......................................54
Chapter Eight... 59
What's Next for the 01 Series.....................59
Conclusion... 65

Introduction

Imagine standing at the edge of a new era, where machines don't just process information, but truly understand and solve some of the most intricate problems humanity has ever faced. That moment is here, and it's embodied in the latest leap forward from OpenAI: the o1 models. These aren't just incremental improvements over their predecessors. No, this is something more—this is the birth of machine intelligence that operates with an intellectual depth previously reserved for human minds.

The release of the o1 model family doesn't merely represent another chapter in the ongoing story of AI development. It's the turning point, the moment when artificial intelligence moves from following instructions to reasoning, from answering questions to solving riddles that have puzzled scientists, mathematicians, and researchers for years. With their ability to perform at levels previously unimaginable, o1 Preview and o1 Mini are not just tools; they're pioneers of a new frontier in thinking.

What makes this moment groundbreaking isn't just the model's ability to generate text or perform simple tasks. We've seen that before. The o1 models venture far beyond, diving into fields like quantum physics, advanced mathematics, chemistry, and biology, handling problems that require deep, multi-layered reasoning—problems so complex that even experts in these domains struggle with them. OpenAI has designed these models to operate at what can only be described as PhD-level intelligence, ushering in an AI capable of not just assisting, but collaborating on tasks that demand extreme cognitive depth.

This book takes you inside that moment. We'll journey through the intricacies of the o1 models, breaking down their unprecedented capabilities, and exploring how they're reshaping industries from healthcare to scientific research, and beyond.

You'll discover not only what these models can do today, but also what they promise for tomorrow—a future where machines assist in solving the unthinkable, freeing human minds to push even further.

Welcome to the dawn of something extraordinary.

Chapter One

The Evolution of AI Technology

Artificial intelligence has been on an incredible journey, with each step pushing the boundaries of what we thought possible. When OpenAI introduced GPT-4, it marked a major leap forward in generating text, answering questions, and engaging in conversations. GPT-4 became a tool that revolutionized industries and empowered countless developers and researchers. But as AI evolved, the need for something even more advanced became clear. The world needed a model that could not only process information but understand it, reason through it, and solve complex problems with precision. That's when OpenAI began developing the o1 models.

The shift from GPT-4 to the o1 series represents more than just an upgrade—it's a paradigm shift in how we think about machine intelligence. While GPT-4 excelled at producing text and interacting in conversations, its limitations became evident when faced with highly specialized, multi-step tasks. For instance, complex areas like quantum physics, mathematical proofs, or advanced scientific research required deeper reasoning, something GPT-4 wasn't built to handle at a high level. The o1 models were created to bridge this gap.

OpenAI designed the o1 series with a very specific goal in mind: to tackle the kind of challenges that require more than just surface-level understanding. These models don't just respond—they reason, analyze, and break down problems in ways that mimic human experts in fields like science and engineering. This isn't just another version of GPT, repurposed for tougher tasks; it's a re-imagining of what AI can do when it is focused on solving the unthinkable.

What sets the o1 models apart from their predecessors is the depth of their reasoning abilities. At the forefront of this revolution is the o1 Preview, a model capable of performing at what can only be described as PhD-level intelligence across multiple domains. It's built to tackle the toughest of problems, the ones that demand more than just computation—they require logic, multi-step thinking, and an advanced understanding of complex concepts. From solving problems in the International Mathematics Olympiad to assisting researchers in developing quantum physics experiments, o1 Preview is reshaping the landscape of what AI can achieve.

Alongside o1 Preview, the more streamlined o1 Mini model offers impressive capabilities at a more affordable scale. While it may not match its sibling's raw power, o1 Mini is still designed to handle intricate tasks like coding, debugging, and problem-solving with efficiency, offering a robust alternative for those seeking advanced AI without the full investment.

This evolution from GPT-4 to o1 reflects not just a technological advance but a fundamental rethinking of what AI can achieve. It shows that AI can now move beyond language generation into areas of high-level reasoning and problem-solving, paving the way for future breakthroughs in science, technology, and beyond.

The journey of artificial intelligence has been a fascinating one, marked by decades of innovation and gradual transformation. In the early days, AI was a concept confined to theoretical discussions, a distant vision of machines that could think, learn, and adapt like humans. Early AI systems were limited to performing specific tasks, often requiring explicit instructions to function properly. It wasn't until the development of machine learning techniques that AI truly began to evolve, learning from data rather than relying solely on predefined rules. This advancement laid the foundation for the creation of models that could recognize patterns, solve problems, and even make decisions.

As AI matured, OpenAI emerged as one of the leading forces in its rapid development. Founded with the mission of ensuring that artificial general intelligence benefits all of humanity, OpenAI has been at the forefront of pushing the boundaries of machine intelligence. Its groundbreaking work in natural language processing and the development of the GPT series of models revolutionized how we interact with AI. The GPT models weren't just another set of tools; they represented a fundamental shift in what machines could do. For the first time, AI wasn't just capable of following orders; it could engage in meaningful conversations, generate creative content, and process complex language structures.

The release of GPT-2 and GPT-3 caught the world's attention, showing that AI could produce human-like text and hold conversations that felt natural. These models had a massive impact, enabling developers, businesses, and researchers to leverage AI for a wide range of applications. From customer service chatbots to content generation, the GPT series changed the game. GPT-4, the latest in that series, brought even more impressive capabilities, improving the fluency and accuracy of text generation while expanding the scope of tasks it could handle.

But while the GPT models revolutionized language generation, it became clear that there were limitations when it came to handling complex, domain-specific problems. Tasks that required deep reasoning, intricate problem-solving, or multi-step processes remained beyond the reach of even GPT-4. Recognizing this need for more advanced AI, OpenAI began working on the o1 series, setting out to create models that could not only understand and respond to language but also solve complex problems in fields like mathematics, physics, and scientific research.

The o1 models represent the next step in AI's evolution. They aim to surpass the success of the GPT series by focusing on specialized tasks that require high-level reasoning. OpenAI's role in advancing machine intelligence has always been about pushing the boundaries of what's possible, and the o1 models are a testament to that mission. These models are designed not just to interact with language but to engage with the deepest intellectual challenges, offering a glimpse of the future where AI doesn't just assist in human endeavors—it becomes an integral part of solving humanity's most complex problems.

Through its continuous innovation, OpenAI has shown that AI can grow beyond its initial capabilities, evolving into something far more powerful. The transition from GPT to o1 isn't just about improving AI performance; it's about redefining the role of AI in specialized fields, proving that the potential of machine intelligence is only just beginning to unfold.

Chapter Two

What Makes the o1 Models Unique

The uniqueness of the o1 models lies in their extraordinary ability to break down and solve complex problems that extend far beyond simple tasks or surface-level analysis. While earlier AI models excelled at generating text, summarizing information, or answering common questions, the o1 models are designed to operate on an entirely different level. They are built to tackle high-level academic problems, where deep reasoning and a multi-step approach are essential.

In fields like physics, mathematics, chemistry, and biology, problem-solving isn't just about understanding a question and responding to it. These disciplines often require synthesizing a vast array of data, working through intricate steps, and applying abstract concepts that go beyond typical computation. The o1 models are equipped with the capacity to navigate these layers of complexity, making them powerful tools in domains that demand precision and depth.

For instance, take the field of quantum physics, where the o1 models have shown the potential to assist in solving equations that would otherwise require significant time and effort from human researchers. Quantum physics is notorious for its complexity, with multi-variable equations that demand an advanced understanding of both the mathematical frameworks and physical laws governing particles at the subatomic level. The o1 models can parse through these equations, analyzing variables, and helping physicists arrive at solutions faster than previously possible.

In mathematics, the o1 models have demonstrated remarkable proficiency by solving problems presented in international competitions such as the International Mathematics Olympiad (IMO). These competitions involve problems that require multiple steps of logical deduction, critical thinking, and mathematical creativity. While previous models like GPT-4 could handle a portion of these tasks, the o1 models were specifically designed to excel in this domain, with o1 Preview solving a significant majority of the problems it was presented with. The model's ability to think through complex mathematical procedures mirrors the intellectual approach of highly trained mathematicians.

Beyond mathematics and physics, the o1 models have also shown promising capabilities in fields like chemistry and biology. In chemistry, researchers often rely on AI to predict molecular behavior or to assist in the discovery of new compounds. The o1 models take this one step further, allowing for more accurate predictions in chemical reactions and interactions, helping chemists explore new possibilities in drug discovery or materials science. In biology, where the analysis of massive datasets is routine, the o1 models assist by sifting through genetic sequences, identifying patterns that may lead to breakthroughs in understanding diseases or developing new treatments.

This high-level academic performance stems from the o1 models' advanced architecture, which enables them to reason through problems step-by-step, much like an expert in the field would. Rather than simply producing an answer based on immediate data, these models can think through the entire process, ensuring that each step logically follows the last. This multi-step reasoning is what sets them apart from previous AI models and allows them to handle tasks that were previously thought to be too complex for machines.

In real-world applications, this ability has the potential to revolutionize research and development in countless fields. Whether it's assisting a physicist in calculating the behavior of quantum particles, helping a mathematician work through a complex proof, or aiding a biologist in analyzing genetic data, the o1 models stand at the forefront of AI's capability to solve problems that were once deemed too difficult for machines to grasp. By breaking down these complex challenges, the o1 models are not just tools—they're collaborators in the pursuit of scientific and intellectual advancement.

The term "PhD-level intelligence" may sound like a bold claim, but with the o1 models, it's grounded in actual performance and real-world applications. This isn't just a marketing tagline—it's a reflection of the models' ability to handle tasks that require deep, multi-step reasoning and intellectual rigor, much like the advanced thought processes of a highly trained researcher. While previous AI models, like GPT-4, could generate text and solve simpler problems, the o1 models are specifically designed to push boundaries in ways that resemble the expertise of a human with an advanced academic background.

What does PhD-level reasoning mean in practice? In many scientific and academic fields, solving problems isn't just about providing an answer. It involves breaking down the problem, considering different variables, exploring multiple pathways, and refining conclusions based on an evolving understanding of the data. The o1 models excel in this kind of advanced reasoning, working through problems in physics, mathematics, biology, and chemistry with the same attention to detail and logical progression that a PhD researcher might exhibit. This is more than just the ability to process data; it's the ability to think critically, challenge assumptions, and produce meaningful, well-reasoned solutions.

One of the most striking examples of the o1 models' advanced capabilities comes from their success in the International Mathematics Olympiad (IMO), a globally recognized competition known for its incredibly challenging problems. These problems aren't just difficult—they require creative thinking, multi-step logical deductions, and a deep understanding of mathematical principles. While GPT-4 managed to solve some of these problems, the o1 Preview model took it to another level, solving 83% of the tasks presented, a remarkable achievement that places it alongside human competitors who have spent years honing their mathematical skills. This isn't an isolated case either; across multiple benchmarks, the o1 models consistently outperformed their predecessors, validating the claim of PhD-level intelligence.

What makes the o1 models truly groundbreaking is not just their success in high-level tasks, but how they achieve it. Unlike simpler AI models that might produce an answer by recognizing patterns or using pre-learned responses, the o1 models engage in what can be described as reasoning. They approach problems much like a human researcher, considering the problem from multiple angles, running through potential solutions, and refining their approach as new information becomes available. This ability to reason through problems is critical in fields where answers are not straightforward and require a deeper understanding of context and detail.

In real-world scenarios, this kind of reasoning has vast implications. Imagine a physicist working on a complex experiment in quantum optics. They might need to develop intricate mathematical models to test their hypothesis, a task that could take weeks or even months of painstaking calculations. With the help of the o1 models, those same calculations could be worked through in far less time, allowing the physicist to focus more on the experimental design and less on the tedious aspects of problem-solving. The o1 models become a tool not just for speeding up processes, but for augmenting human expertise, offering insights that could take humans much longer to generate.

This extends to fields like chemistry and biology as well. Researchers often need to parse through enormous datasets, identify patterns, and develop theories that can be tested in a lab. The o1 models can assist by analyzing these datasets with a level of reasoning that approaches human intelligence, offering researchers a way to refine their hypotheses and test ideas more efficiently.

The true power of PhD-level reasoning in the o1 models is how it mirrors human thought processes, pushing AI beyond rote problem-solving and into the realm of advanced intellectual collaboration. By breaking down and reasoning through the most complex problems, the o1 models represent a new frontier in artificial intelligence, proving that machines can engage with academic challenges in ways that were once thought to be purely the domain of human intellect.

Chapter Three

Applications Across Disciplines

Revolutionizing Scientific Research

The introduction of the o1 models marks a turning point in scientific research, where artificial intelligence begins to operate not just as a tool, but as an integral part of the investigative process. These models are designed to assist in some of the most complex research tasks that would typically demand an immense amount of time, effort, and specialized expertise. The o1 models bring their PhD-level reasoning to these challenges, aiding researchers by generating mathematical formulas, analyzing data, and refining scientific hypotheses.

In fields like quantum optics, where the understanding of particle behavior at the subatomic level is crucial, the need for advanced mathematical modeling cannot be overstated. Typically, physicists would spend weeks or months developing complex equations to test their hypotheses, often working through multiple iterations to ensure precision. This process is slow, meticulous, and prone to human error. The o1 models step in here, not as mere calculators, but as collaborators. They are capable of reasoning through these equations, testing different variables, and offering solutions in a fraction of the time, allowing physicists to focus on the broader experimental framework and theory.

Take, for example, a situation where a researcher is exploring the behavior of light particles in a vacuum. This type of work demands intricate quantum mechanical calculations. The o1 models can assist by generating the necessary equations, running through potential outcomes, and even suggesting refinements to the hypothesis based on real-time analysis of the data. This frees researchers from the often tedious work of trial and error, allowing them to push their theories further and faster.

In chemistry, the o1 models have shown their value in predicting molecular interactions and chemical reactions. Research in this field often requires the exploration of how different compounds will behave under various conditions, a task that relies heavily on detailed simulations and computational models. With the o1 models, chemists can analyze potential reactions, predict the outcomes of molecular interactions, and even assist in discovering new compounds for applications like drug development or materials science. Their reasoning ability means they don't just provide outcomes—they offer a deeper understanding of why certain interactions happen and suggest pathways that might not have been immediately obvious.

The impact of o1 extends into biology as well, particularly in fields like genomics and bioinformatics. Biological data sets are vast, and finding patterns within them requires a blend of computational power and nuanced reasoning. The o1 models are capable of parsing through these immense datasets, identifying connections between genetic markers, and offering insights into the mechanisms of diseases. For instance, when analyzing genetic mutations related to cancer, the o1 models can help identify which specific changes in the DNA sequence are most likely to contribute to the disease, offering researchers a clearer path to potential treatments. The ability to rapidly generate hypotheses, test them against biological data, and refine them based on results is game-changing for researchers working in fields where time and accuracy are critical.

In each of these fields, the o1 models are more than just assistants—they act as advanced co-researchers, providing the reasoning power needed to accelerate discoveries. By handling complex data analysis and problem-solving tasks, the models allow scientists to focus on the more creative aspects of their research, driving innovation forward at a pace that was previously unimaginable. This shift is revolutionizing how research is conducted across disciplines, proving that artificial intelligence can be a powerful ally in tackling the world's most pressing scientific questions.

The o1 models' ability to assist in refining scientific hypotheses, generating mathematical formulas, and analyzing data across quantum physics, chemistry, and biology shows just how adaptable and valuable they are in the realm of complex academic research. The future of scientific discovery is no longer limited by human capacity alone—AI is becoming a key player in pushing the boundaries of what we can achieve.

The Role in Healthcare

The o1 models hold remarkable potential in revolutionizing healthcare, where the ability to process and analyze vast amounts of data is critical to breakthroughs in treatment and research. Healthcare professionals and researchers often grapple with enormous datasets, from patient records and genomic sequences to medical imaging and clinical trial results. The o1 models bring an advanced level of reasoning and analysis to these tasks, helping medical experts uncover insights that were previously buried under mountains of complex data.

One of the most promising areas for o1's application is in the field of cell sequencing. Understanding the genetic code of cells has become crucial in identifying the root causes of diseases, particularly in cancer research and personalized medicine. Cell sequencing generates massive amounts of genetic data, requiring advanced algorithms to interpret the mutations, patterns, and variations in DNA. The o1 models have the capacity to analyze these sequences, identifying critical genetic markers more efficiently and accurately than traditional methods. Their advanced reasoning abilities allow them to make connections between genetic variations and specific diseases, offering researchers the opportunity to develop more targeted treatments.

Another area where o1 models shine is in medical imaging. The interpretation of images like MRIs, CT scans, and X-rays is a field that demands both precision and speed, particularly in diagnosing conditions such as tumors, fractures, or organ abnormalities. These tasks often involve analyzing thousands of images to detect subtle signs of disease progression. The o1 models can process these images at a scale and accuracy level that far exceeds human capabilities. By identifying minute details that might be missed by the human eye, these models can assist radiologists in making faster, more accurate diagnoses, ultimately leading to earlier interventions and better patient outcomes.

In drug discovery, the complexity of analyzing chemical compounds and predicting their interactions with biological systems has always been a major bottleneck. Developing a new drug involves testing countless combinations of molecules to find one that is both effective and safe for human use. This process can take years, if not decades, using traditional methods. The o1 models, however, can significantly accelerate this process by simulating chemical interactions and predicting the efficacy of drug compounds. By analyzing vast libraries of molecular structures and cross-referencing them with known biological interactions, the models can help researchers identify promising candidates for further testing, potentially shaving years off the drug development timeline.

Moreover, the o1 models aren't just tools for speeding up research—they contribute to a deeper understanding of complex medical problems. For example, in a clinical trial setting, the models can analyze patient data in real-time, offering insights into how certain drugs affect specific populations or even predicting which patients are most likely to respond positively to a new treatment. This level of analysis, which blends data processing with advanced reasoning, could transform personalized medicine, allowing for more precise treatment plans tailored to individual genetic profiles and medical histories.

The implications of the o1 models in healthcare are profound. They can help clinicians and researchers uncover patterns in data that would otherwise go unnoticed, leading to faster diagnoses, more effective treatments, and ultimately, better patient outcomes. From accelerating the pace of drug discovery to improving the accuracy of medical imaging, these models represent a significant leap forward in the ability of artificial intelligence to assist in saving lives. The potential of o1 in healthcare is not just about speed—it's about using AI to unlock new insights that could fundamentally change how we understand and treat diseases.

Chapter Four
Coding and Multi-Step Workflows

In the realm of programming, the o1 models have proven to be game-changers, particularly when it comes to handling complex coding tasks, debugging, and automating multi-step workflows. Unlike previous models, which primarily assisted with simple tasks like code generation or answering technical questions, the o1 models bring a new level of sophistication and precision to the table. These models are capable of reasoning through the logic behind coding problems, understanding the structure of the code, and identifying potential errors or inefficiencies that may not be immediately obvious.

For developers, this means that the o1 models can be deployed not just as code generators, but as collaborators in the programming process. They can assist with tasks that involve multiple steps, such as writing, debugging, and refining code across different platforms or applications. A developer working on a large project might need to integrate various systems, write complex algorithms, and ensure that everything functions seamlessly. The o1 models can automate portions of this workflow, significantly reducing the amount of manual effort required. By streamlining these processes, developers can focus on more creative and critical aspects of their projects rather than getting bogged down in the details of code execution.

Debugging, a notoriously time-consuming aspect of coding, is another area where the o1 models excel. Debugging involves not just finding the source of an error, but understanding how the entire system interacts and where something has gone wrong in the logic or syntax. The o1 models can comb through large codebases, identify bugs, and even suggest solutions in a fraction of the time it would take a human developer. This ability to catch errors early in the development process not only saves time but also reduces the risk of costly mistakes making it into production environments.

In addition to their performance in general coding tasks, the o1 models have demonstrated exceptional abilities in coding competitions, where their reasoning and problem-solving skills are put to the test against some of the best human coders in the world. One of the most notable examples of this is their performance on platforms like Codeforces, a competitive programming site where coders from around the globe solve algorithmic challenges under time constraints. In these competitions, o1 Preview placed in the 89th percentile, a remarkable achievement that ranks it among the top coders globally. This ranking isn't just a reflection of the model's ability to generate code; it showcases its deep understanding of multi-step logic, optimization, and efficient problem-solving—skills that are critical in competitive programming.

The implications of such performance are vast. For developers working on high-stakes projects, from software development to AI-driven applications, the o1 models offer a powerful ally. Their ability to handle complex coding tasks efficiently, reduce errors through advanced debugging, and optimize workflows can dramatically shorten development cycles and enhance the quality of the final product. Whether a developer is creating a large-scale enterprise system or working on a groundbreaking algorithm, the o1 models provide a new level of support, allowing for faster, more reliable outcomes.

Moreover, the o1 models' capacity to handle coding in a highly competitive environment further solidifies their role as indispensable tools for both individual developers and larger teams. By automating repetitive tasks and offering insights into complex problems, they free up developers to focus on innovation, enabling the creation of more sophisticated and polished applications in less time.

The future of programming is not one where AI replaces developers, but one where AI, like the o1 models, becomes a critical collaborator in the process of building the software and systems that will define the next wave of technological advancement.

Chapter Five

The Economic Divide: Preview vs. Mini

When comparing o1 Preview and o1 Mini, it becomes clear that while both models belong to the same cutting-edge family, they are designed with different strengths and use cases in mind. Each model brings its own unique advantages, catering to different needs based on performance requirements and cost considerations. While o1 Preview represents the pinnacle of what OpenAI's new series can achieve, o1 Mini is a more streamlined, cost-effective solution that still maintains remarkable problem-solving capabilities.

The o1 Preview model stands out for its unmatched performance, especially in complex, high-level tasks that require advanced reasoning. Built to operate at a PhD-level across multiple disciplines, o1 Preview excels in areas like quantum physics, advanced mathematics, and deep scientific research. Its ability to tackle intricate, multi-step problems makes it the go-to model for researchers, developers, and professionals who need AI to handle highly specialized tasks with precision and depth. Whether it's generating complex mathematical equations or reasoning through dense scientific hypotheses, o1 Preview is designed to perform at the highest level, pushing the boundaries of what AI can accomplish.

However, such extraordinary capabilities come at a higher cost. o1 Preview is a more resource-intensive model, requiring more processing power and a larger investment for access. This makes it ideal for users or organizations that demand top-tier AI for specialized projects where the stakes are high, and precision is paramount. Enterprises, academic researchers, and those working on cutting-edge technological innovations are the primary users of o1 Preview, as the investment in its advanced problem-solving capabilities pays off in terms of breakthroughs and efficiency.

On the other hand, o1 Mini offers a more accessible, cost-effective option without sacrificing too much in terms of performance. While it doesn't match the sheer processing power of o1 Preview, o1 Mini is still an impressive model, especially when it comes to handling coding tasks and mathematical problems. It offers around 80% of the capability of its larger sibling, but at a fraction of the cost, making it an attractive choice for individuals or smaller teams who need a robust AI solution without the financial burden of the full-powered model.

In coding, o1 Mini continues to stand out as a highly capable assistant. It can handle complex debugging tasks, generate efficient code, and automate multi-step workflows with a high degree of accuracy. For many developers, o1 Mini offers everything they need to streamline their coding processes, identify errors early, and maintain high-quality standards in their work. Despite its lower cost, the model's reasoning and problem-solving capabilities in programming are impressive, offering a solution that balances affordability with performance.

In mathematical applications, o1 Mini holds its own as well. While o1 Preview may dominate in highly specialized academic fields, o1 Mini is perfectly suited for handling advanced mathematical problems, especially those that require logical deductions, multi-step processes, or optimization. Whether it's assisting with calculations in finance, engineering, or basic research, o1 Mini proves itself to be a versatile tool that can still perform remarkably well in tasks where accuracy and speed are essential.

Ultimately, the choice between o1 Preview and o1 Mini comes down to the user's specific needs and budget. For those requiring the absolute best in terms of reasoning, problem-solving, and advanced intellectual capacity, o1 Preview is the obvious choice. Its unparalleled performance in specialized fields makes it the perfect tool for groundbreaking research and development. Meanwhile, for developers, small businesses, or individuals who want access to powerful AI without the premium cost, o1 Mini provides a cost-effective yet capable alternative, maintaining much of the sophistication of its larger counterpart, especially in areas like coding and math.

In summary, both models represent a significant leap forward in artificial intelligence, but they cater to different segments. o1 Preview leads in high-stakes environments where precision and complexity rule, while o1 Mini ensures that cutting-edge AI remains accessible to a broader audience, proving that powerful AI solutions don't always need to come with a hefty price tag.

Choosing between o1 Preview and o1 Mini depends on the specific demands of the task at hand and the resources available. Each model has its strengths, and understanding when to leverage the power of o1 Preview or the efficiency of o1 Mini can make all the difference in optimizing both performance and cost-effectiveness.

For professionals working on highly complex and specialized tasks, o1 Preview is the ideal choice. This model's ability to handle intricate multi-step reasoning makes it perfect for situations where deep intellectual engagement is required. Researchers in fields such as quantum physics, chemistry, or advanced mathematics, for instance, will find o1 Preview indispensable when solving problems that require complex calculations, modeling, or the synthesis of vast amounts of data. Its performance in generating mathematical formulas or simulating experiments goes beyond what any earlier AI models could achieve, making it the right tool for cutting-edge academic or scientific research. If the task involves developing new theories, conducting experiments that demand precise and high-level computation, or tackling problems previously deemed too complex for AI, o1

Preview is the model that offers the power necessary to drive breakthroughs.

For developers working on large-scale software projects or managing complicated multi-system integrations, o1 Preview is also the best choice. Its advanced capabilities in coding and debugging allow it to not only generate code efficiently but also to understand and resolve complex logic errors across various programming environments. It excels in automating workflows that involve multiple steps, reducing development time and minimizing the risk of costly mistakes. If the project demands exceptional performance, such as in high-stakes coding for critical systems or enterprise-level software, o1 Preview's investment pays off through increased efficiency and fewer errors in the final product.

However, not every project requires the full power of o1 Preview, and this is where o1 Mini shines as a cost-effective, yet highly capable, alternative. o1 Mini is ideal for professionals who need robust problem-solving without the premium investment. For example, developers working on medium-scale applications, startups, or smaller teams can rely on o1 Mini to handle most coding tasks, from writing and debugging code to automating repetitive workflows. Its ability to perform well in coding tasks, while being significantly more affordable, makes it an attractive option for developers who don't require the top-tier features of o1 Preview but still need a reliable AI assistant to improve productivity.

In research environments where the task at hand involves data analysis, routine mathematical problems, or less computationally intensive tasks, o1 Mini offers more than enough capability. It's particularly suited for researchers working in fields like finance, engineering, or data science, where the problems are complex but not as domain-specific or intricate as in fields like quantum physics. o1 Mini can efficiently process datasets, generate insights, and assist with problem-solving in mathematical contexts, proving to be a strong partner for those looking to balance performance and cost.

For professionals looking to integrate AI into their workflows without needing cutting-edge reasoning power, o1 Mini is an excellent fit. It provides solid capabilities in coding and math while offering a more manageable cost structure, making it ideal for developers, small businesses, and independent researchers who want access to high-performance AI without the need for deep specialization.

In summary, when choosing between o1 Preview and o1 Mini, the decision hinges on the complexity of the task and the level of investment that makes sense for the user. o1 Preview is designed for those who need the absolute best in AI-driven reasoning, whether they're solving advanced scientific problems or managing large-scale development projects. On the other hand, o1 Mini provides a versatile, cost-effective option for those who need solid AI performance but don't require the full capabilities of its more powerful counterpart. By aligning the model choice with the specific needs of the project, professionals, researchers, and developers can maximize both the effectiveness and the value of the o1 models.

Chapter Six

Limitations and Drawbacks

While the o1 models represent a significant advancement in artificial intelligence, they come with some limitations that are important to consider, especially for certain user groups. The most notable limitation is that, at this stage, the o1 models are restricted to text-based tasks. Unlike previous iterations like GPT-4, which offer features like browsing and image generation, the o1 models currently focus exclusively on solving complex textual problems. This constraint limits their applicability in fields where visual data is crucial, affecting users such as content creators, designers, and professionals who rely heavily on multimedia outputs.

For content creators and designers, who often use AI for generating visuals, brainstorming graphical concepts, or even creating interactive media, this limitation presents a clear challenge. While the o1 models excel at reasoning through complex text-based problems, they can't generate images or process visual information, which means these users might find the models less useful for their day-to-day creative tasks. Similarly, professionals in fields like architecture, product design, or marketing may find the absence of browsing and image creation capabilities restrictive, especially when they need real-time data or visual elements for their projects. These users often require a more holistic AI that can handle both text and visuals to generate more comprehensive results.

Another significant drawback is the usage cap currently imposed on the o1 models. At this stage, OpenAI limits the usage of o1 Preview to 30 messages per week and o1 Mini to 50 messages per week for most users. For individuals who need consistent and long-term access, particularly researchers and developers engaged in ongoing projects, these restrictions can be quite limiting. In research and development workflows, continuous access to AI is often critical. Researchers working on experiments or developers building software applications require the ability to engage with the models frequently, running numerous iterations to refine their work. The weekly message limits slow down the workflow, potentially delaying progress and hindering the efficiency gains the o1 models offer.

Despite these drawbacks, OpenAI has been transparent about the current limitations and has promised future updates that will address some of these issues. Browsing capabilities, image generation, and file uploads—features already present in GPT-4—are expected to be incorporated into the o1 models in future iterations. This would expand the functionality of the models significantly, allowing content creators, designers, and professionals working with visual data to integrate the models into their workflows seamlessly. Furthermore, OpenAI is also expected to revise the usage caps, potentially offering more flexibility in the near future as they continue to test and refine the models. These improvements would make the o1 models more versatile and accessible to a broader audience.

In the meantime, users who require extensive, unrestricted access to AI or who rely heavily on multimedia features may find that GPT-4 remains a better fit for their current needs. The o1 models, while exceptional in handling complex text-based tasks, are still evolving, and these constraints may prevent them from being the all-in-one solution for certain professions at this moment.

However, it's important to keep in mind that OpenAI's roadmap for the o1 models suggests that these limitations are temporary. As the models mature and gain additional features, they will become more adaptable and robust, allowing them to serve a wider variety of use cases. For now, users will need to evaluate their specific needs and determine whether the advanced text-based reasoning of the o1 models outweighs the current limitations in their particular field of work.

Chapter Seven
Safety and Security

One of the most significant advancements in the development of the o1 models lies in the realm of safety and security. As artificial intelligence becomes more capable, the risks associated with its use also grow, making it crucial to ensure that models like o1 perform within safe and ethical boundaries. OpenAI has taken proactive steps to enhance the safety features of the o1 models, and these efforts have yielded promising results. During rigorous safety tests, particularly in avoiding unsafe or inappropriate content generation, the o1 models have demonstrated notable improvements compared to their predecessors.

One of the most critical aspects of these safety tests is the models' ability to resist "jailbreaking" attempts—situations where users try to manipulate the AI into producing harmful or controversial content. In such tests, the o1 Preview model scored

84 out of 100, a significant leap compared to GPT-4's score of 22. This indicates that the o1 models are much better equipped to follow safety guidelines and avoid generating content that could be considered harmful or inappropriate. This improvement reflects OpenAI's commitment to building AI systems that are not only more intelligent but also more aligned with ethical and safety standards.

To further strengthen AI safety, OpenAI has partnered with several global AI safety institutes, including organizations in both the United States and the United Kingdom, to rigorously test and evaluate the o1 models before they are released to a broader public. These collaborations are essential, as they allow for a more comprehensive understanding of the potential risks associated with these advanced AI systems. Through these partnerships, OpenAI is working to ensure that the o1 models are designed with multiple layers of safety and that they are tested under diverse scenarios to avoid unintended consequences.

However, despite these advancements, ensuring the long-term safety of AI models like o1 remains an ongoing challenge. While the current safety measures are effective, AI safety is a constantly evolving field, and new risks may emerge as these models become more integrated into various industries and applications. Continuous oversight is essential to keep up with the potential risks, and OpenAI acknowledges the importance of regularly updating safety protocols to address new threats as they arise.

The key to maintaining AI safety is a commitment to iterative improvement. As the capabilities of models like o1 expand, so too must the systems that regulate their use. OpenAI has made it clear that they will continue to prioritize safety in future updates, refining the models to better adhere to safety standards while simultaneously enhancing their functionality. This means regularly assessing the models for vulnerabilities, ensuring they cannot be easily manipulated, and implementing safeguards to prevent misuse in real-world applications.

One of the potential risks with highly advanced AI models is their use in generating misinformation or malicious content. Even with robust safety measures in place, there's always a chance that these models could be used in ways that were not originally intended. This is why continuous research and testing are so crucial. OpenAI, along with its global partners, is dedicated to addressing these risks by ensuring that the models remain aligned with ethical guidelines and that their outputs stay within the bounds of safe, responsible use.

At the same time, OpenAI is working to strike a balance between safety and usability. While it's essential to minimize risks, it's equally important that the models remain accessible and functional for the professionals, researchers, and developers who rely on them. The goal is to create AI that is not only powerful and versatile but also secure and aligned with the values of the communities it serves.

In conclusion, while the o1 models represent a significant leap in AI capabilities, their safety and security features have also made impressive strides. By prioritizing safety in development and working closely with global AI safety institutes, OpenAI is ensuring that these models are equipped to handle the complex ethical challenges posed by advanced artificial intelligence. However, this is just the beginning. As AI continues to evolve, so too must the efforts to ensure its safe, responsible, and ethical use. The future of AI safety depends on constant vigilance, ongoing research, and a commitment to refining the boundaries of what these powerful systems can and cannot do.

Chapter Eight

What's Next for the o1 Series

As groundbreaking as the current o1 models are, OpenAI has made it clear that we are only scratching the surface of what this new series can achieve. The o1 models, in their current form, focus primarily on text-based tasks, but OpenAI's roadmap promises a future rich with enhancements that will vastly broaden their capabilities. Some of the most eagerly anticipated features include browsing capabilities, file uploads, and image generation—functionalities that are already present in the GPT-4 models but are absent in o1 for now.

The addition of browsing capabilities would allow the o1 models to access real-time information, making them more versatile for research and data gathering. This would be a game-changer for professionals who rely on up-to-date data, allowing the o1 models to pull information from the web, analyze it, and provide insights within the same session. The ability to browse would also enable the models to assist in more interactive and dynamic tasks, where up-to-the-minute accuracy is crucial.

File uploads are another feature in development that will allow users to provide documents, datasets, or other materials directly to the o1 models for analysis. This capability would significantly enhance the o1 models' utility in fields like finance, legal analysis, and research, where professionals often need to work through extensive files or datasets. Instead of relying solely on input via text, users would be able to upload their own materials and have the models process them for insights, summaries, or deeper analysis.

Image generation is another key feature that is expected to revolutionize fields such as design, content creation, and marketing. Currently, o1 models are limited to text-based outputs, but integrating image generation will allow for creative collaboration in industries that rely on visual content. For designers, this means being able to work with AI to brainstorm new ideas, generate unique visuals, and prototype design concepts. Content creators and marketers will be able to leverage the models to create compelling imagery that complements their written content, further streamlining the creative process.

These upcoming features aren't just incremental updates—they represent a significant expansion of the use cases for the o1 models. In industries where real-time data analysis, multimedia creation, and large-scale document processing are essential, the future capabilities of the o1 models will redefine how professionals approach their work. From architects sketching out new building concepts to data analysts pulling insights from massive datasets, the addition of these features will extend the reach of the o1 models into new, exciting territories.

One of the most interesting aspects of OpenAI's strategy is its commitment to maintaining both the

GPT and o1 series as separate, but complementary, families of models. While the o1 models excel at solving complex, specialized problems, they are not designed for the general-purpose tasks that GPT-4 handles so well. GPT-4 remains essential for users who need a versatile, conversational AI that can handle a wide variety of tasks, from content generation and casual conversation to summarization and customer service applications. Its strength lies in its adaptability to different contexts, making it a go-to for users who need an all-purpose AI assistant.

On the other hand, the o1 series is laser-focused on more advanced problem-solving, particularly in fields that require deep reasoning, multi-step thinking, and specialized knowledge. OpenAI's dual approach ensures that users have the right tool for the right job. When a task requires domain-specific intelligence—whether it's quantum physics, coding optimization, or complex mathematical modeling—the o1 models are the natural choice.

Their ability to reason through complex problems with a depth that GPT-4 cannot match makes them indispensable for researchers, developers, and professionals working on high-level challenges.

By continuing to develop both series, OpenAI is catering to a broad spectrum of users. Whether someone needs an AI model that can engage in everyday tasks or one that can tackle the most challenging academic problems, OpenAI ensures that their suite of models covers the full range of needs. The dual approach also allows for specialization within industries, with GPT models continuing to serve as general-purpose assistants, while the o1 models carve out their role as experts in solving the unthinkable.

Looking forward, the continued evolution of the o1 series promises to open even more doors. As browsing, file uploads, and image generation are introduced, the models will become more versatile and essential across a wider range of fields. OpenAI's vision for the future is not just about creating smarter machines, but about expanding the capabilities of AI to solve problems that, until now, were beyond the reach of both humans and machines.

In conclusion, the future of the o1 series is bright, with upcoming features poised to make these models even more powerful and adaptable. Whether it's revolutionizing content creation, improving real-time data analysis, or enabling complex problem-solving in niche fields, the o1 models are set to reshape how we interact with AI. At the same time, OpenAI's commitment to maintaining both the GPT and o1 series ensures that users will continue to have access to the right tool for any task, making AI an even more integral part of professional and creative endeavors in the years to come.

Conclusion

The introduction of the o1 series has undoubtedly redefined the landscape of artificial intelligence. These models have pushed past the limitations of their predecessors, not only in terms of performance but in their ability to tackle some of the most complex and specialized problems across multiple fields. The o1 models represent a new era in AI, where machine intelligence begins to resemble human-level reasoning in its ability to process, understand, and solve intricate tasks. From revolutionizing scientific research to transforming the way we approach healthcare, programming, and beyond, the o1 series has set a new standard for what AI is capable of achieving.

In science, the o1 models have already proven themselves as indispensable tools. Their ability to handle multi-step reasoning and solve high-level problems has accelerated discoveries in fields such as quantum physics, chemistry, and biology. For researchers, the o1 models are not just assistants—they are collaborators, helping to refine hypotheses, generate complex mathematical formulas, and analyze massive datasets. This kind of intellectual partnership between AI and human researchers is reshaping the future of innovation.

In healthcare, the o1 models are unlocking new possibilities in areas like cell sequencing, medical imaging, and drug discovery. Their capacity to analyze vast amounts of medical data and draw meaningful insights can lead to faster diagnoses, more precise treatments, and a deeper understanding of diseases. The models' potential to revolutionize personalized medicine is enormous, as they contribute to more efficient, targeted care that could save lives and improve outcomes for patients worldwide.

As the o1 models continue to evolve, their influence will extend into every corner of technology and beyond. The promise of upcoming features—like browsing capabilities, image generation, and file uploads—signals that the o1 series will soon become even more versatile, breaking down barriers in industries such as design, content creation, and real-time data analysis. With these advancements, the models will transcend their current role in specialized problem-solving, becoming essential tools in a wider array of professional environments.

Looking to the future of AI, the possibilities seem endless. Machine intelligence is poised to continue evolving, with each new development bringing us closer to the goal of artificial general intelligence. As models like o1 become more advanced, their role in society will expand, from transforming industries to solving the world's most complex problems. We can expect AI to drive innovation in ways we have yet to fully imagine, leading to breakthroughs that were once considered out of reach for human intelligence alone.

The enduring role of machine intelligence in shaping the future is clear. As AI continues to improve, it will not only assist us in solving existing challenges but also help us to uncover entirely new opportunities for progress. The o1 series is just the beginning of this journey, a glimpse into a future where humans and machines work together to push the boundaries of knowledge, technology, and possibility. This new era of collaboration between human intellect and machine intelligence promises to unlock unprecedented levels of innovation, driving progress in science, technology, healthcare, and beyond.

www.ingramcontent.com/pod-product-compliance
Lightning Source LLC
Chambersburg PA
CBHW070411230526
45471CB00006B/2752